Pat's Perfect Pizza

Written by F. R. Robinson
Illustrated by Sarah Beise

Pat makes pizza.

She puts pickles in the pan.

She puts peanuts in the pan.

She puts peppers in the pan.

Pat puts popcorn in the pan.

People say, "What a mess!"

But Pat says, "It's perfect!"